Mel Bay Presents

ADVANCED FIDDLING

Solos, Instruction & Technique

Includes: Orange Blossom Special, Under the Double Eagle, Sally Goodin, & more!

GW00514870

By Craig Duncan

A stereo cassette tape of the music in this book is now available. The publisher strongly recommends the use of this cassette tape along with the text to insure accuracy of interpretation and ease in learning.

ACKNOWLEDGEMENTS

I want to thank Greg Jennings for his guitar work and Gordon Reid for his assistance in recording and mastering this project, Les Leverett and WSM for the photographs, Susan Duncan for her hours of typing and assistance, Bill Bay, Dean Bye and the folks at Mel Bay Publications for their assistance, and the many fiddlers whom I have listened to and based arrangements on in preparing this book.

ABOUT THE AUTHOR

Craig Duncan is an active Nashville musician who spans the gap of both the country and classical music fields. He began his professional music career in Charlotte, North Carolina where he worked as fiddler, vocalist and bassist. After moving to Nashville, Craig began working as a fiddler and vocalist at Opryland, U.S.A. In addition to performing at Opryland, he did shows such as the Porter Wagoner Show, the Canadian National Exhibition in Toronto, Canada, and various conventions throughout the country.

In September of 1978 Craig went to work on the Grand Ole Opry with Wilma Lee Cooper, as fiddler and vocalist. He performed weekly on the Opry and did TV specials such as the Grand Ole Opry TV Special, the Bluegrass Spectacular with Tom T. Hall, and Good 'N Country with Jean Shepard and Justin Tubb. Also during this time he began working with a string section in Nashville doing commercial recordings and performing in A.F. of M. orchestras throughout the Nashville area. Craig went back to work for Opryland in 1980, performing with a contemporary country group. Along with his performance activities, Craig is Artist/Teacher of Fiddle at the Blair School of Music in Nashville, holding a Master of Arts degree, and a writer of fiddle method books for Mel Bay Publications.

TABLE OF CONTENTS

INTRODUCTION

This book has been written for two purposes. The first is to present some of the more popular fiddle tunes to the fiddler who has already begun developing his technique. The tunes and licks presented in this book are intended to be used as a source from which to draw. Because of the aural tradition of fiddling, the tunes found here are played in many different ways. It has been the intent of the author to determine a somewhat standard way of performing these tunes and also to offer typical variations.

The second purpose of the book is to offer a follow-up to the book entitled Deluxe Fiddling Method - Mel Bay Publications, 1980. In the Deluxe Fiddling Method, the basics of fiddling are covered, along with 49 tunes in the keys of A, D, G and C. The Advanced Fiddling Method covers additional tunes in these keys and also presents five more keys as well as cross tuning and show tunes.

A special note needs to be made concerning bowings. The markings in this book can offer only one possibility of bowing the many different tunes. In many instances, it has been very difficult to decide on one bowing pattern as the best possibility. Although many of the bowings marked may be the best way to play a particular passage, there are instances in which the fiddler should use his own judgement and find the most comfortable bowing for his style.

The overall intent of the book is to help carry on the great tradition of American fiddling. This music, which has been such an important part of our heritage, should continue to thrive and reach a larger and larger audience.

KEY OF F

The key of F has one flat, B♭. It is notated at the beginning of the line
like this:

There are three finger patterns used in the key of F. The finger pattern on the G and D strings is the same as the pattern for the D and A strings in the key of C. There is a low second finger, B♭, on the G string, and a low second finger F on the D string. It looks like this:

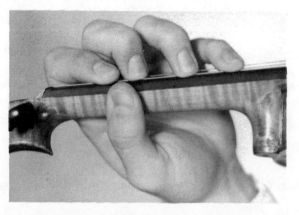

The finger pattern on the A string has the first finger against the nut with the remaining fingers a whole step apart. This is the same as the E string pattern in the key of C. It looks like this:

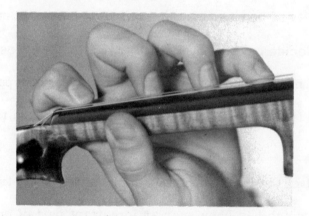

The finger patter on the E string is the same as for the A string except the fourth finger is played low, next to the third, so that the pitch becomes a B♭. It looks like this:

Here is a diagram of the notes in the key of F.

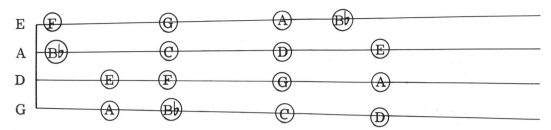

FISHER'S HORNPIPE

This tune is often played in the key of D, but is presented here in its original key of F. It was originally known as Fischer's Hornpipe for its writer.

The third part presented here is an addition to the tune which was used by Eck Robertson in the early 1920's. It begins in third position with the first finger on the A. The shift back to first position takes place in measure 19.

LONDONDERRY AIR

This old tune is known by two names, the most common of which is Danny Boy. It stems back to the tradition of fiddlers of the British Isles performing airs as well as hornpipes, jigs, reels, etc.

The arrangement presented here begins with a single string simple melody which should be played with long, full bow strokes. The verse of the tune goes through the downbeat of measure 16, with the chorus beginning on the second beat of measure 16, and lasting through the downbeat of measure 32. The key of F is an excellent key for the use of double stops, therefore an arrangement with double stops is found in measures 32-64 typical of the style of many fiddlers.

9

Craig Duncan

BEAUMONT RAG

Beaumont Rag is a traditional fiddle tune consisting of a sixteen measure theme with variations. The first variation (measures 16-32) is an example of adding notes around the melody. The bowing of the variation is of particular interest as it changes back and forth between the Georgia shuffle and the regular style shuffle.

The second variation (measures 33-48) begins in fifth position (first finger C on the E string), and continues in fifth position through measure 44. This is accomplished by anchoring the first finger in position and using it as a reference point for the other fingerings. The shift back to first position in measure 44 should be done while the open A string is being sounded.

The third variation (measures 49-64) utilizes the cross shuffle bowing on the C and F chords. The original theme may also be played with double stops as in the fourth variation (measures 65-80). A D is added to the C7 chord in measures 65 and 73, causing it to become a C9 chord.

Another possibility for shuffling the bow is found in the fifth variation (measures 81-96). It involves beginning up bow and slurring to the pitch below and back to the original pitch, and then rocking the bow from the higher strings to the lower strings.

1 2 3 Remain in Postion

KEY OF B♭

The key of B♭ has two flats, B♭ and E♭. It is notated at the beginning of the line like this:

There are three finger patterns used in the key of B♭. The pattern for the G string has a low second finger, the same as in the key of F. It looks like this:

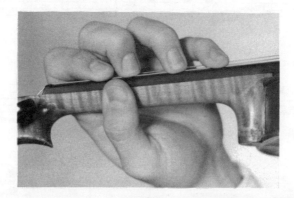

The finger pattern on the D string has the first finger against the nut, with the remaining fingers a whole step apart. It looks like this:

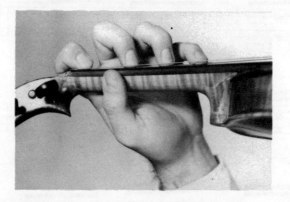

The finger pattern on the A and E strings is the same, with the first finger against the nut and the fourth finger low. It looks like this:

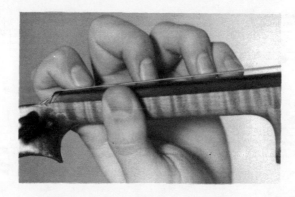

Here is a diagram of the notes in the key of B♭.

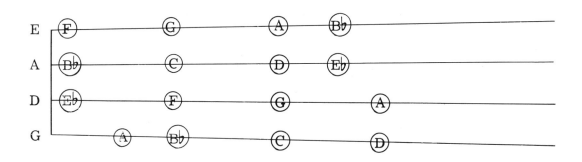

RED LION HORNPIPE

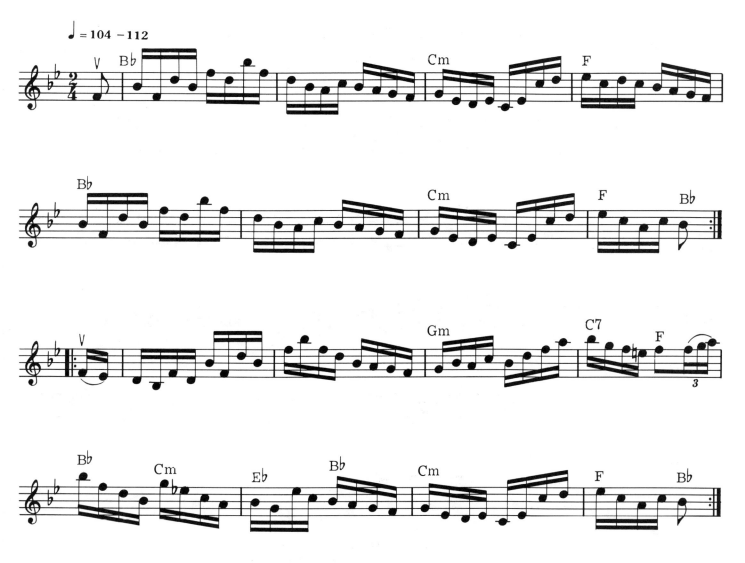

DONE GONE

This arrangement of Done Gone comes from many sources. Measures 1-9 are based on arrangements by Charlie Collins, Earl White and Kirk McGee. Measures 10-17 are also played by Collins and White, but not by McGee. This part must be a later addition to the tune, as many other fiddlers omit it. The third part and its repeat (measures 18-33) make up a standard section to the tune. A Kenny Baker rendition was used as a basis for the the variations on part one found in measures 34-49. Baker omits the second part and goes directly to the G minor section in measure 50. Measure 65 repeats to measure 34. At the conclusion of measure 48 the Coda is played.

HIGHLAND HORNPIPE

Highland Hornpipe was originally a two part tune, the first part in the key of B♭, and the second in the key of F. The more modern version presented here is based on a rendition by Texas fiddler, Dave Ferguson. The notes of the first two sections, which are the original parts, have been slightly altered to allow for a smoother flow in the melodic line. At measure 19 the first part is stated again, followed by a variation in measures 27-34. Measures 35-42 present a contrasting section in the key of G minor. The first part then reappears in measures 43-50. Measures 51-59 present a final variation on the first part. This is followed by a restatement of the second part and a final statement of the first part with a two measure tag.

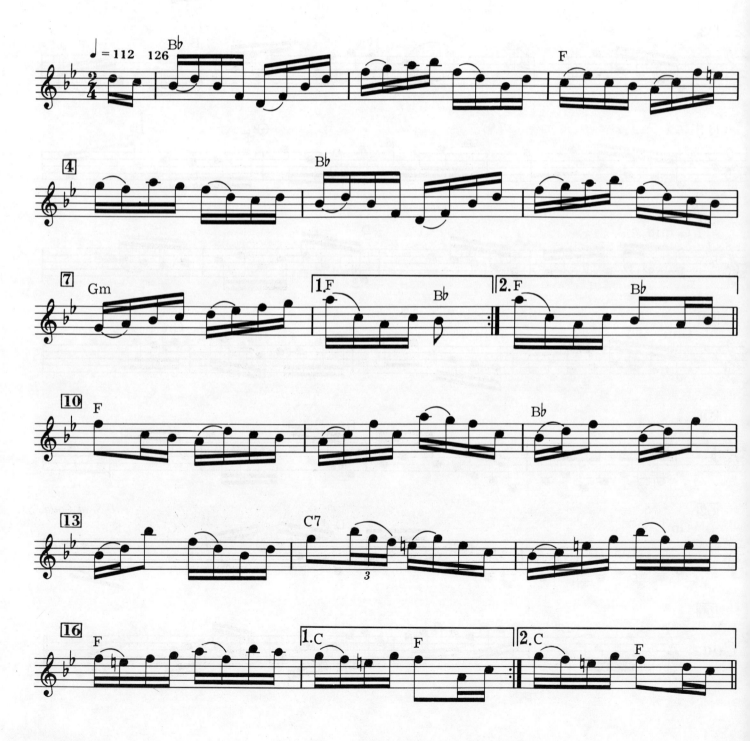

Kenny Baker & Bill Monroe

KEY OF E MINOR

The key of e minor has one sharp, F♯, the same as the key of G major, therefore the finger patterns for e minor are the same as those for G major. The difference in the two keys is found in which pitch the music centers upon. Tunes in the key of G will usually end on a G, as tunes in e minor will usually end on an E. There is also a more frequent use of the accidental D♯ in the key of e minor than in the key of G. D♯ is known as the leading tone in the key of e minor as it is only one half step lower than E and tends to "lead" upward to E.

KEY OF E MAJOR

The key of E major has four sharps, F♯, C♯, G♯, and D♯. It is notated at the beginning of the staff like this:

There are three finger patterns used in the key of E. The finger pattern on the G string starts with the first finger about an inch from the nut and has a whole step between each finger. The first finger may also be moved back to the nut to play the pitch G♯, which is also in the key of E.

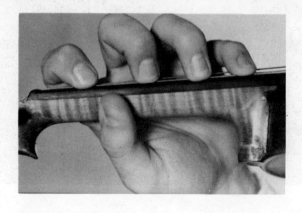

The finger pattern on the D and A strings is the same, with the first finger about an inch from the nut, the second and third fingers a whole step each apart, and the fourth finger a half step from the third.

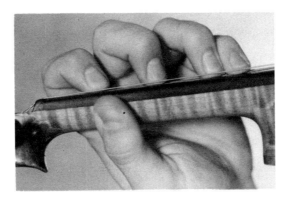

The finger pattern on the E string has the first finger about an inch from the nut, the second finger a whole step up, the third finger a half step up, and the fourth finger a whole step higher than the third finger.

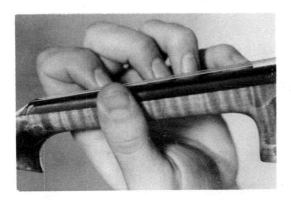

Here is a diagram of the notes in the key of E.

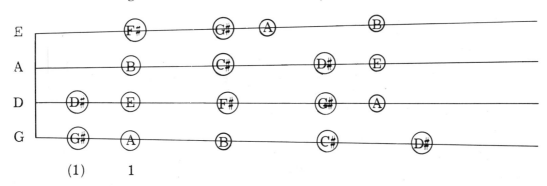

Notice that the G♯ on the G string and the D♯ on the D string can be played with a low first finger.

23

SAY OLD MAN

The full name for this tune is Say Old Man Can You Play the Fiddle? This version comes from an East Tennessee fiddler, Smokey White. The tune consists of eight parts. The first three parts, measures 1-8, 9-16, and 17-20, are in E minor. The fourth and fifth parts, measures 21-28 and 29-32, are in E major. The sixth and seventh parts, measures 33-36 and 37-41, complete the tune in E minor. Measures 41-42 are to be retarded continuously until the final harmonic E. The accompaniment should stop on the E minor chord in measure 41 and then sound a final E minor chord when the last note is being sustained.

THE DRUNKEN WAGONEER

The Drunken Wagoneer is similar to Say Old Man in that it changes between E minor and E major. The first part (measures 1-8) is in E minor. The second part (measures 9-16) is in E major. The third part (measures 17-24) begins in E major but moves back to E minor in measures 23-24 for the repeat of the first part.

COOLEY'S REEL

This two part tune has the same chordal structure for both parts. It is based on an E minor scale with an occasional C#. The triplets found throughout the tune are typical of its Irish background.

KEY OF A MINOR

The key of a minor has no flats or sharps, the same as the key of C major. The finger patterns are also the same as for C major. The difference in the two keys is that music in the key of C centers around C and music in the key of a minor centers around A. The leading tone in the key of a minor is G# and therefore there are usually more G#'s in the key of a minor than in the key of C.

STAR OF THE COUNTY DOWN

This is a relatively obscure waltz in the tradition of the British Isles. It can either be played in a slow three or with a feeling of one beat per measure as indicated here. The tune consists of two 16 measure sections and is then repeated with a double stop variation. The last four measures (61-64) are then repeated (measures 65-68) to end the tune.

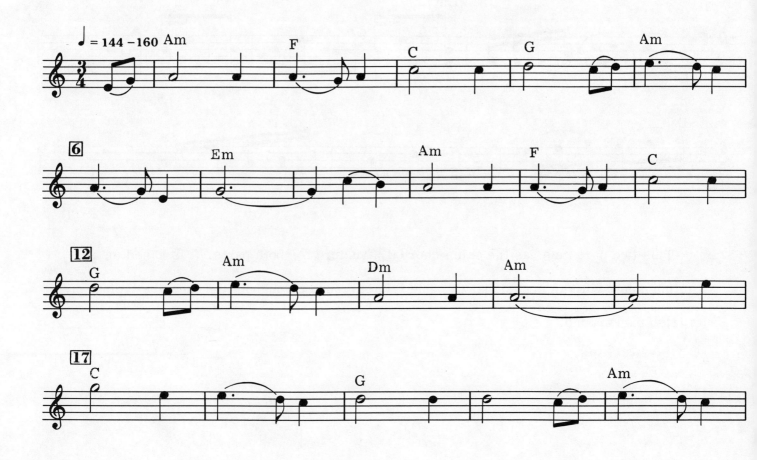

28

CATTLE IN THE CANE

Cattle in the Cane is a two part fiddle tune, one part in a minor and one part in mixolydian mode on A (major scale with flat seventh). Practice the bowing to the first part so that it flows very smoothly. You should notice in measures three and four the combination of the two types of shuffle. The E in measure seven can be played with third finger, followed by a slide to third finger D.

Measures 18-66 are taken from a rendition by Texas fiddler Terry Morris. Measures 18-33 and 50-65 are variations on the original eight measure theme. Measures 34-49 present a different part centered in E minor. As is usual among Texas fiddlers, much of the tune is played with separate bow strokes.

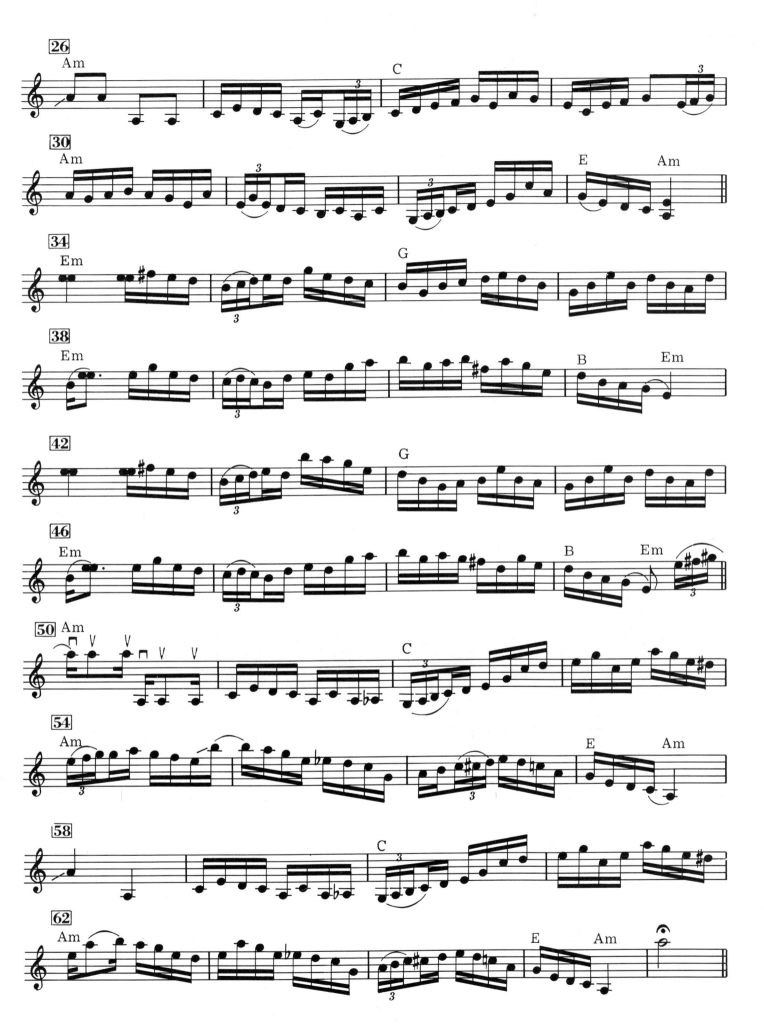

SHOW TUNES

Listen to the Mockingbird

Listen to the Mockingbird is one of the most famous fiddle tunes because of its bird calls. The first section of the tune should be played in a relaxed manner. The first part is stated in measures 1-8 and then varied in measures 9-16. The chorus is stated in measures 17-24. A tremolo variation on the first part is found in measures 25-40.

Measures 41-54 make up the "trick" section of the tune. At this point, the fiddler runs the left hand up and down the string in very high position in imitation of birds chirping and singing. Another common way to make bird calls is to move the left hand to the G string side of the fiddle and place the fingers on the strings near the end of the fingerboard. A very effective way to produce bird calls is to have the left hand in this position with the fingers holding the G string and the thumbnail against the string sliding back and forth. The bob-white and whippoorwill are often imitated as well as any other birds the fiddler may know. The woodpecker is also comically imitated by knocking the wooden part of the bow against the side of the fiddle.

Upon completion of the bird call section, the closing licks in measures 54-56 are added and the rhythm stops in measure 56. The fiddler then starts again at a much faster tempo, with the rhythm instruments joining in at measure 57. The next eight measures are a statement of the original melody at the new tempo. A variation on the chorus is found in measures 65-72. Measures 73-80 make up a variation on the first part, beginning with a very common lick in measures 73-80. The arrangement is ended with a cross shuffle variation (measures 81-88) and the final measures concluding with a D major tag.

ORANGE BLOSSOM SPECIAL

The Orange Blossom Special is a fiddle tune which no two fiddlers play the same. In fact, it is seldom played the same way by one fiddler. Therefore, the arrangement presented here should be used as an outline and a source from which to draw, rather than as <u>the</u> way to play Orange Blossom Special.

The tune incorporates three basic sections. They are: 1. Train imitations and "hot licks," 2. Cross shuffle bowing, and 3. Melodic section. The tune is in the key of A, although the E chord is predominant throughout. The guitar (or other instrument) usually introduces the tune as indicated. The fiddle then enters with imitations of a train whistle (measures 1-6, 9-13). Measure 7 is an imitation of the train bell. Measures 19-22 present an often used lick, as well as measures 23 and 30. The x's in measures 31-42 are to be played with the left forefinger on the notes indicated as the bow is moved up and down the length of the strings. This is a percussive imitation of the clickety-clack of the train on the track. The bow should not move perfectly parallel with the strings, but should also move slightly across the strings, allowing the pitches to be audible. The left hand pizzicato indicated in these measures should be omitted until this bowing technique is mastered. Measures 47-50 perform the important function of alerting the rhythm section of the chord change coming in measure 51. The train imitation section, regardless of its length, is ended with a four measure lick similar to the one found in measures 47-50. Another example of a similar lick is found in measures 166-169.

Measures 53-68 comprise the cross shuffle bowing section. The first six measures utilize the original shuffle pattern with string crossings. The cross or double shuffle begins in measure 59 and continues through measure 67. Measure 68 ends the shuffle section and prepares for the melodic section beginning in the following measure. Measures

63-64 are written with a D7 chord (C♮'s), as this has come into common use. Of course the D chord as fingered in measures 55-56 could also be used. Other shuffle patterns may also be used on the chords found in measures 53-68. Many amateur fiddlers use the following pattern:

This pattern should be avoided as it sounds very amateurish.

The melodic section is found in measures 69-84. It contains a rather straightforward melody played with the shuffle bowing.

Another section of train imitations begins in measure 85. The licks presented in measures 121-127, 138-141, and 142-147 were taken from various renditions of the Orange Blossom Special by Vassar Clements. Measures 148-155 present a different type of cross shuffle bowing which begins up bow. The groups of three slurred notes are performed by sliding the fingers flat and then back up to pitch. When the chords change in measures 150, 152, and 154, the fingers slide down a whole step and back up a half step. Measures 156-163 utilize the same chordal progression with the original cross shuffle bowing. As mentioned earlier, measures 166-169 are a four measure lick ending the train imitation section.

The cross shuffle section returns in measures 172-187. The melodic section reappears in measures 188-203 with small variations. The tune is then ended in the key of A with a four measure tag.

ORANGE BLOSSOM SPECIAL

by Ervin T. Rouse

40

TUNINGS

Fiddle tunes are often played with the fiddle tuned to pitches other than the standard GDAE. The use of other tunings creates new possibilities for harmonic and melodic development as well as an opportunity for the fiddler to work within a different framework.

The tunings used usually consist of notes taken from a major chord. One of the more popular tunings is AEAC# (low to high). By tuning the G and D strings up to A and E, and the E string down to C#, the open strings form an A chord. This tuning is used for the arrangement of Lost Indian presented on page 43. Another chord oriented tuning is DDAD. The G and E strings are tuned down to D, thus emphasizing D as the tonal center. This tuning is used for the arrangements of Dry and Dusty on page 44 and Bonaparte's Retreat on page 47.

Two other tunings which should be mentioned are AEAE and GDGD. They allow the fiddler to use the same fingerings in two different octaves and therefore have been favorite tunings of many novice fiddle players. The AEAE tuning has often been referred to by old time fiddlers as "high bass" because the G and D strings are tuned a whole step higher. The GDGD tuning is used for the arrangement of Drunken Hiccups found on page 46.

Although the tunings mentioned here are the most frequently used, there are many other possibilities. The tunes presented here are written to be played as if the fiddle had not been retuned, therefore many of the written pitches will not be the pitches which are sounded.

LOST INDIAN

This is one of several tunes bearing the title Lost Indian. This particular tune is common among Texas fiddlers. It is a three part tune presented with an extra variation on the second part (measures 13-20). These measures may be omitted to make each part the same length. All of the parts share the same harmonic structure. A closing tag has been added to give an example of an ending that can be used with this tuning.

DRY AND DUSTY

Dry and Dusty is an old time fiddle tune which uses the open D tuning. This arrangement is based on a Benny Thomasson rendition. The first part is stated in the first four measures and then repeated with slight variation. Measures 9-16 make up the second part. The third part (measures 17-24) is similar to the second. The fourth part uses the two low D strings in octaves. The first part returns in measures 33-40. The second and third parts are stated an octave higher in measures 41-56. The final part (measures 57-64) adds a hint of b minor. The last two measures are simply a tag.

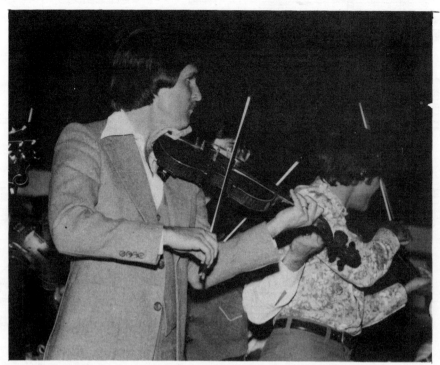

Craig Duncan

Tater Tate

Contest Style Accompaniment

The way in which contest tunes are accompanied has been influenced by "western swing." In this style the bass line and accompanying chords change on every beat. Most of the contest style tunes will work with this style of accompaniment.

Two patterns are presented here, either of which may be transposed to work in other keys. There are many variations on these patterns, therefore the two presented here should be taken as representations of the style.

The first pattern presented is the one the author used in the companion cassette recording of this book.

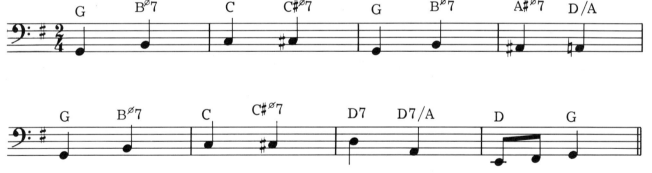

DUSTY MILLER

Dusty Miller is one of the standard "hot" breakdowns. It consists of four basic parts which are varied and repeated. This arrangement was based on renditions by Jimmy Mattingly and Byron Berline.

The first part is eight measures long, followed by an eight measure variation. The second part, measures 17-24, is also followed by a variation. The third part, measures 33-40, is repeated without variation. The fourth part is played in third and first positions with the shifts taking place while playing the open E string.

The variations beginning in measure 57 are the same four basic parts as played by Byron Berline. Measures 57-72 make up the first part, measures 73-88 the second part, measures 89-104 the third part, and measures 105-120 the final part.

The bowing style for this type fiddling is quite varied, hardly ever using a consistent pattern, or even the same bowings every time the tune is played. Therefore, the bowings marked are stylistic examples rather than necessary phrase markings.

GREY EAGLE

This arrangement of Grey Eagle contains five parts with variations and a final statement in double stops of the first part. It is based on renditions by Howdy Forrester, J.B. Prince, Smokey White and Dave Ferguson.

The first part is a straightforward statement of the theme. The second part, measures 11-18 alternates between first and third positions. A variation of this part follows in measures 19-26. The third part, measures 27-34, begins in third position with shifts back and forth between first and third positions while the open E string is sounding. The following variation on this part, measures 35-42, is done in the same manner. The fourth part is found in measures 43-50, followed by a variation in measures 51-58. The fifth part is one of the most distinguishing parts of this tune with its run up to the E harmonic and back down to the low A on the G string. The section is found in measures 59-66 followed by a fancy variation in measures 67-74. The first part is used to conclude the tune, followed by a four measure tag.

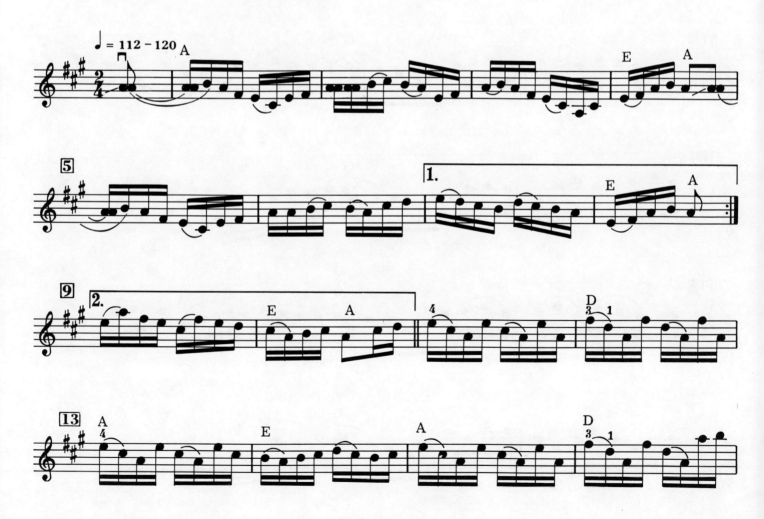

LEATHER BRITCHES

Leather Britches is a traditional southern fiddle tune. This arrangement is based on a Howdy Forrester rendition. Note the bowing pattern of the first eight measures. It gives a lilt to the tune and may also be used in other contexts to provide this type rhythmic accent. The lick on the second beat of measure 8 occurs several times throughout the tune and should be noted as a typical phrase ending. It is to be done with emphasis on the double stop so that it sounds "heavier" than the preceding notes. Measures 26-29 are to be played in third position. The next section begins in third position, moves to first in measure 33, back to third in measure 34 and returns to first position during the open A on the second half of the second beat of measure 35. Measures 38-45 involve the use of drones (open G or D strings). This is accomplished by shifting up and down the D string in measures 38, 39, 40, 42, and 43. The shift from first to third position should be from first finger E to first finger G. The shift back down takes place when the open D string is sounding on the first beat of each measure.

The chordal structure for measures 5-7, 22-24, 42-44, and 50-52 presented on pages 74-75 is accepted as the standard pattern, although this particular chordal pattern is not implied by the melodic movement. Another pattern which has been used and comes closer to the implications of the melody is as follows:

measures 5-8

This pattern can also be used in measures 22-24, 42-44, and 50-52. Whichever pattern is chosen should be used consistently throughout the tune.

LEATHER BRITCHES

SALLY GOODIN

Sally Goodin is probably the most popular of all breakdowns. The version presented above includes the two parts on which the many variations are based.

The variations presented here are typical of the style in which Sally Goodin is played. The drone of the fourth finger A on the D string with the open A is characteristic of this tune. Measures 33-35 are to be played in third position, returning to first position on the open strings on the downbeat of measure 36. The same is true for measures 37-39 and measure 40. Measures 49-64 are to be played in first position with the fourth finger extended to play the C♮'s. Measure 65 begins in third position with a fourth finger extension for the high E. It returns to first position on the open A and E of measure 67. The same is true for 69-71. Measure 73 starts in second position as indicated. The slides in measures 74 and 78 should imply the D and G, but should sound as a slide to the C♯ and E rather than be strictly articulated. Measures 81-88 bring the only relief from the monotonous chordal structure. This is a later addition to the tune which has become a standard variation. Measures 89-104 present further Texas style variations on the tune. A stuttering effect should be produced by the bow in measures 105, 107, and 113 by emphasizing the downbeat, giving slight importance to the second sixteen, barely moving the bow on the third and fourth sixteenths and then emphasizing the second beat with a long solid bow stroke.

71

TOM AND JERRY

This arrangement comes from a rendition by Mark O'Conner. It consists of eight parts, each one being eight measures long followed by an eight measure variation. Mark's versions of tunes such as Tom and Jerry have made him a major contest winner throughout the country.

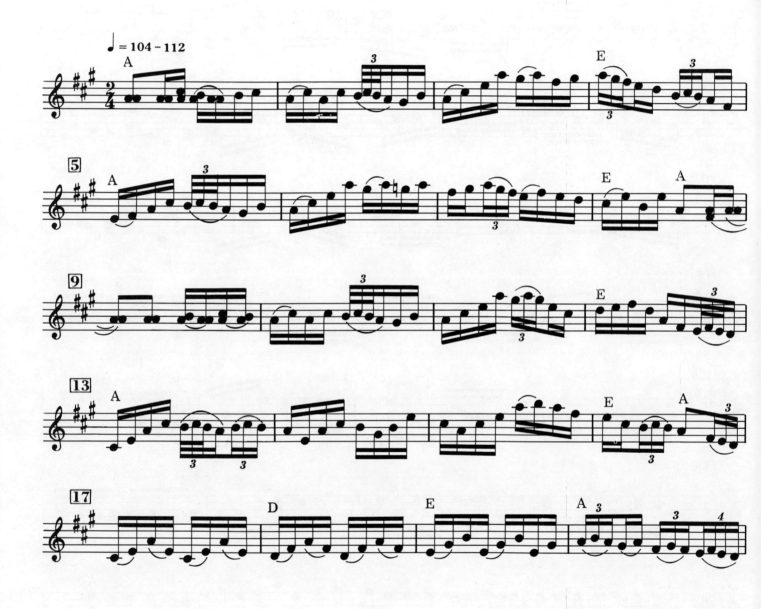

RAGTIME TUNES

Another type of tune which has become popular among fiddlers is the ragtime tune. These tunes give a good basis for improvisation and variation and therefore are often heard in fiddle contests.

BLACK AND WHITE RAG

This is one of the favorite rags among Texas style contest fiddlers. The first part is sixteen measures long in the key of G. The second and third parts are also sixteen measures long each, but are in the key of C. These parts share the same harmonic structure, with the third part functioning as a variation of the second. The tune returns to the key of G for the fourth part which is a restatement of the first part. The next part, which comes from a rendition by Benny Thomasson, provides extra variation to the tune. The main theme then returns to end the tune.

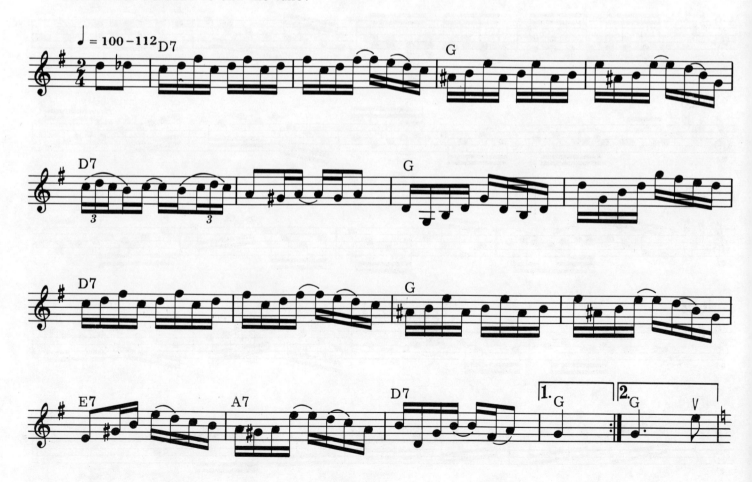

Roy Acuff

CINCINNATI RAG

Cincinnati Rag was once a very popular tune used as a theme song by radio station WLW. It is a two part tune ending on the first beat of measure 32. The next sixteen measures (33-48) are a variation on the first part, based on a rendition by Kenny Baker.

Measures 48-64 are commonly used as a variation on the second part, although the harmonic structure remains the same as part one. The final sixteen measures present a cross (or double) shuffle variation.

X = left hand pizzicato

COTTONPATCH RAG

This is a popular ragtime tune presented with six parts. The first is a standard statement of the theme. The second part is also played by most fiddlers who perform this tune. The third part is a variation of the author's. The fourth part is also a standard variation. Parts five and six are further variations created by the author.

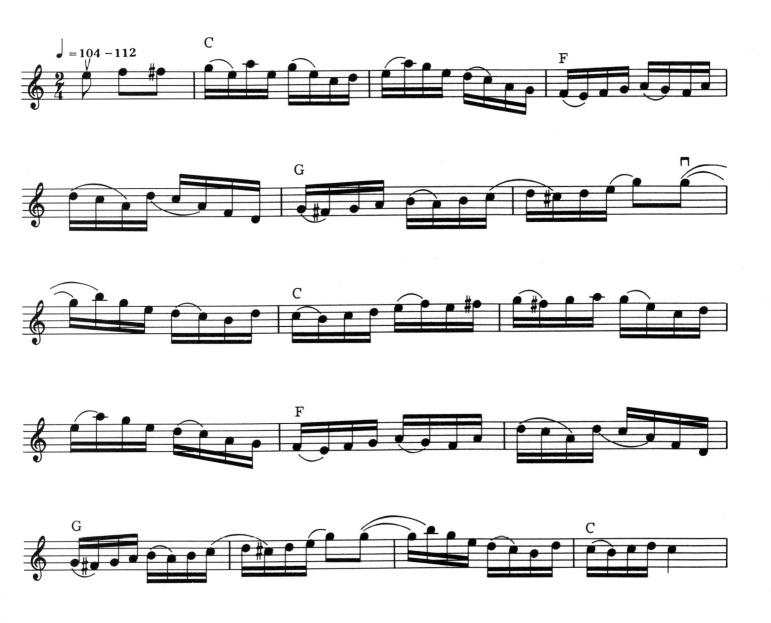

DON'T LET YOUR DEAL GO DOWN

Don't Let Your Deal Go Down is an instrumental derived from a two part song of the same name. This version contains six parts which are variations over the same harmonic structure. Measures 18-19 and 26-27 contain a common bowing pattern which can be used in many situations. Measures 34-49 are similar to measures 49-64 of Cincinnati Rag and can be used interchangeably. Measures 49-65 are a cross (double) shuffle variation. The next variation (measures 66-81) contains a syncopated chordal pattern to be played with a swing feel. Measure 82 is an added measure leading to the repetition of the original theme (measures 83-90). It recurs in measure 91 when the theme is repeated. Benny Thomasson's Texas swing-style fiddling was used as the source for this arrangement.

I DON'T LOVE NOBODY

This is a one part tune, presented with five variations. Mark O'Conner's hot fiddling was the basis for this arrangement.

WILD FIDDLER'S RAG

This arrangement of Wild Fiddler's Rag was based on a rendition by Joe Meadows, a West Virginia fiddler who worked on the Grand Ole Opry for several years. It consists of three parts with a four measure introduction. The slides in measures 22, 23, 26, 27, 30 and 31 are to begin a half step lower than the written pitch, starting on the beat and lasting half the value of the note. The third part (measures 39-55) is in the key of C. A repetition of the first part follows with the first four measures repeated and used as an ending.

Howdy Forrester

ADDITIONAL FAVORITES

JACK OF DIAMONDS

This version of Jack of Diamonds is based on a rendition by Benny Thomasson. It is a two part tune presented with variations. The first part of the tune is eight measures long and is followed by a variation (measures 9-16). The second part (measures 17-24) incorporates the use of triplets typical of the style of Texas fiddlers. Measures 25-32 involve more Texas style licks, providing a variation on measures 17-24. Measures 33-40 and 40-48 are further variations on part one. Measures 49-56 are a repetition of the second part and are followed by a variation which begins an octave lower (measures 57-64). The tune is concluded with a two measure tag.

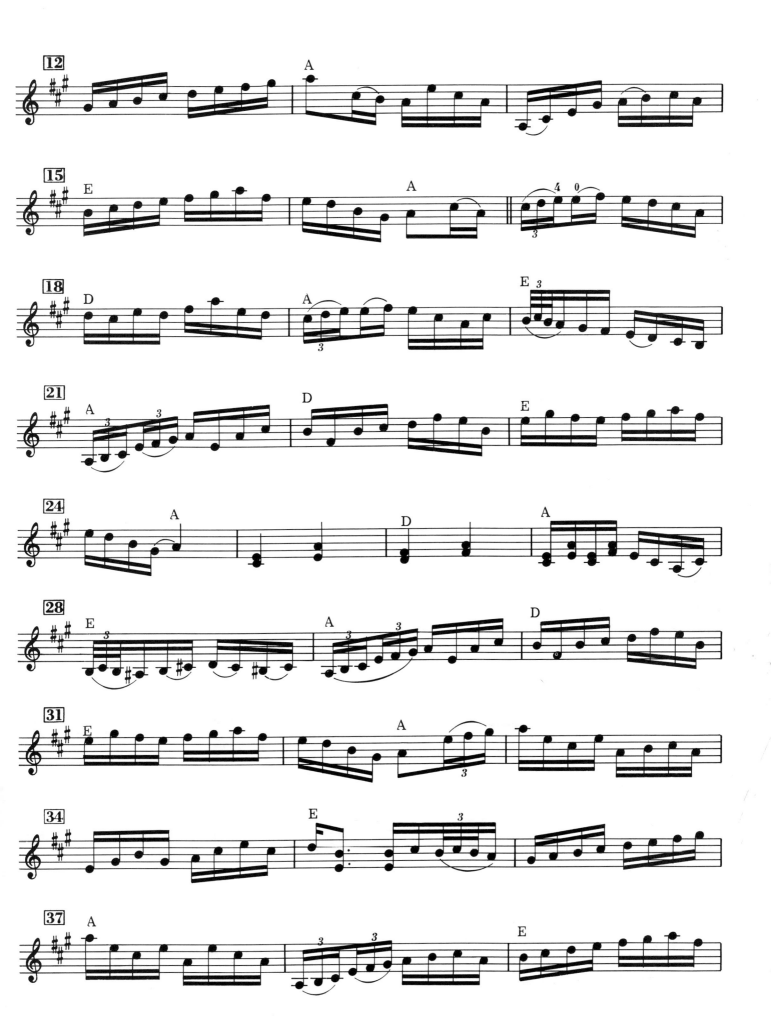

Mark O'Conner

LOST HIGHWAY BLUES

The wild fiddling of Scotty Stoneman was used as the basis for this arrangement of Lost Highway Blues. Scotty, a member of the Stoneman family, was known for his high intensity, energetic fiddle playing.

Measures 51-57 are typical of his style. The chromatic movements in these measures are to be done with the same fingerings as would be used for slides. The actual body of the tune ends at measure 62. The original eight measures are then repeated, followed by a variation (measures 71-78), incorporating parallel fifths, another characteristic of Scotty Stoneman. The following sixteen measures are further variation continuing the use of parallel fifths. The original theme appears in measures 95-102. The double shuffle is then used for a closing variation (measures 103-110). The four measure tag is a further example of Stoneman's use of parallel fifths.

101

102

LOST INDIAN

This version of Lost Indian is based on a rendition by Kenny Baker. This standard southern fiddle tune bears the same name as a tune which is played in the key of A with the fiddle retuned to AEAC♯. The Lost Indian presented here is a favorite among cloggers.

The main part of the tune is presented in measures 1-8. Measures 9-24 make up part two. The harmonic structure is the same for both parts and it should be noted that the second part could be conceived as an embellishment of the first part an octave higher. Measures 25-32 present a variation on part one and measures 33-48 present a variation on part two.

RYE STRAW

There are six parts which make up this tune. It is characteristic of old time fiddle tunes in that much of the tune is centered around the dominant chord (A). The second, third, fifth and sixth sections are examples of this type of harmony. The sixth section acts as a bridge back to the repeat. The tune is then ended, after the repeat of the first three parts, with a very common double tag.

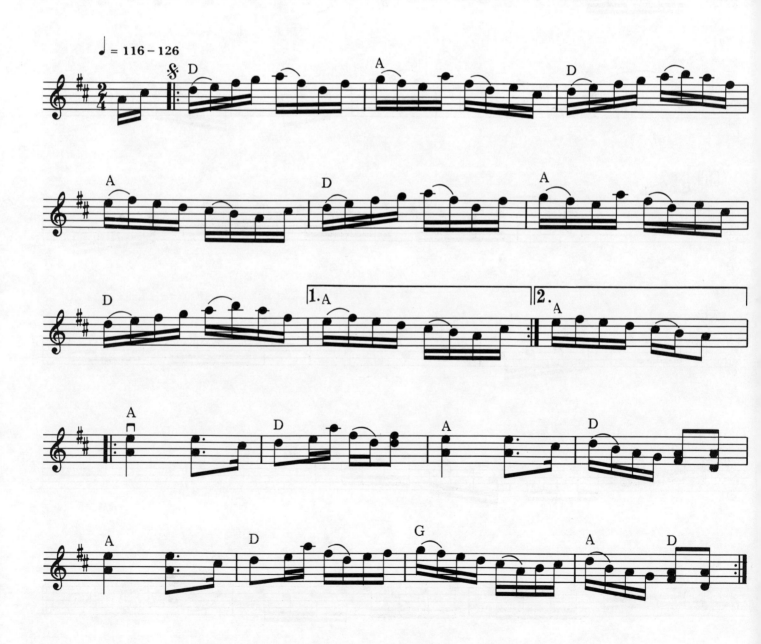

D.S. al Coda

Coda

107

STONEY POINT

This is a two part tune with variations presented on each part. Measures 19-26 are a variation on the first part followed by another variation in measures 27-34. Measures 35-42 are a variation on the second part followed by another variation in measures 43-50. The more common name for this tune among old time fiddlers is Nigger in the Woodpile.

TWINKLE LITTLE STAR

The first version of Twinkle Little Star presented here was inspired by Frazier Moss. Measures 13-14 and 17-18 are to be fingered in fourth position as indicated. The second version presented is based on a Kenny Baker rendition. In this version, the harmonic structure of the second part (measures 43-58) remains the same as the first part (measures 27-42).

Earl's Breakdown, a famous banjo tune by Earl Scruggs, has the same harmonic structure as Twinkle Little Star and the variations presented in measures 59-91 contain Benny Martin style licks which can be used for either tune.

111

TWINKLE LITTLE STAR

Variations

UNDER THE DOUBLE EAGLE

Under the Double Eagle is an old John Philip Sousa march which has become a standard in the fiddler's repertory. The seldom heard introduction is presented in measures 1-17. The main part of the tune begins in measure 17 on the second half of the first beat. The sixteen measure theme ends in measure 33 and a variation follows (measures 33-47). At measure 48 the tune modulates to the key of F. The melody of this part (measures 48-81) is presented with very little embellishment. The following part (measures 82-113) is not heard as often as the two parts which precede it. It is written with considerable embellishment and has the same harmonic structure as measures 48-81. Following measure 113, the tune goes to measures 18-46 and then to the Coda.

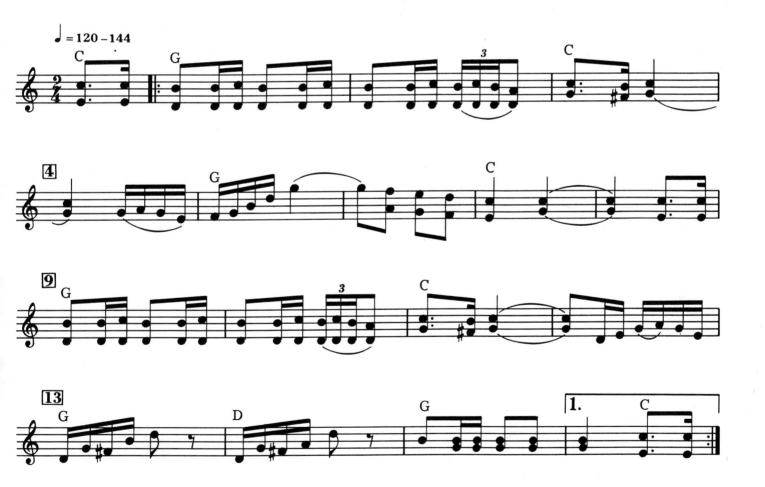

WHISKEY BEFORE BREAKFAST

Whiskey Before Breakfast is a traditional two part tune with the repeat of each part written out as a variation. Further variations are found in measures 33-64.

Everybody's Music Teacher